Woman Undone

Holly Snow

Thank you…

CM, for seeing my light when I couldn't.

MM, for reminding me who I am, and what I've conquered...and for being the reason (you know).

JM, for helping me turn the broken girl into the unbreakable one.

All the love, to infinity and beyond.

Contents

Woman..7

Climbing Mountains............................53

Unbreakable....................................105

Woman

<u>Number One.</u>

Raindrops fall from your clouded eyes and
sunbeams peek through from behind the mountain
curves of your lips.
You are a piece of this world just as much as
anything else.
Dance with the wind and shine with the stars.
Start with yourself when you're counting all of the
beautiful things.

<u>Spoiler.</u>

You think you want to be with him but what you really want is to know that you're going to be okay without him.

Spoiler: you are

<u>For Adah.</u>

I see a lot of myself in you,
the way your mind is stubborn to self-love but so
willing to pour every bit of encouragement into
others...
the way your smile holds uneasiness in who you are
to them but security in who they are to you.
You have a lot to be proud of,
a lot to offer,
you just have to set yourself free.

Words.

I want to write words that stick with people.
I want the words that bleed from the pen in my
hands to be the same words that press into a
person's soul so deeply that they remember them.
I want to write words that you won't forget when
you need to hear them most.

Stuck.

Maybe the reason you can't move is that you keep taking on the weight of everyone else's turmoil while you haven't even picked up your own. You have plenty of time to go back and pick up everyone's burdens, but you have to be unchained of your own first.

<u>Best Seller.</u>

every mark on your body
a different chapter

the tears in your eyes
always a conflict

and the smile on your face
my favorite resolution

you are by far the most
interesting book I've ever read

Affirmation.

babe, you've got a mad good heart
and fire in your soul.
and let me tell you,
not even an ounce of you is worthless.
you never have been.
you never will be.

Revival.

There is revival in the raindrops that live in your
eyes so much of the time.
When you free the pain you've held on to,
you will save the joy from drowning in the ocean of
who you are.

Already Gone - 3:56 a.m.

I am already gone.

All I really am now is just a body with a
few dark thoughts,
but the rest of me is gone - left,
nothing.

And the dark thoughts aren't even me anymore,
someone else has control.

If there is anything I am right now,
it is lifeless.

Somebody, please tell me it's okay to
let go of it all for real this time,
I want to leave now.

Invalidated.

honey, stop letting people invalidate you
your feelings
your thoughts
these are the foundation of your makeup,
they lay out the pieces of who you are

Brooklyn.

she's sitting here across from me and I can see how
at peace she is with a life like this. she's not worried
about anything, and she seems free. she doesn't
want to be held down any longer, by anything or
anyone. she lives this moment to the fullest because
she lives it alone. with herself, and she loves
herself.

<u>Active Love.</u>

They say love can move mountains, but I think I
want a love that climbs mountains.

That sometimes stumbles and needs water every
now and then.

A love that knows how good it is when we choose
to persevere.

I want an active love.

<u>One Year.</u>

my heart feels so stripped down and my bones
beaten in
I can't move, I can't breathe, I can't think
this is the emptiness that makes me feel
overwhelmingly numb
...yes, I feel too much of nothing
and I know this doesn't make any sense, but the
reality is that living every day and wishing you
hadn't, do not go together
except in my world, they do

For Rachael.

It's like you think you've finally found someone you can fully give yourself to, all the pieces you were too ashamed to let others see, and all the parts of yourself that you're not really convinced deserve to be loved yet.

And everything is really good because you think you've found someone you can find a home in, but somewhere along the way they fall short, they take things for granted and make you second guess everything you thought you knew.

I'm sorry these people keep telling you it's okay to let your guard down and then proving to you that your armor was valid.

But you have to know, there is no part of you that is worthless.

You have eyes like the ocean and a laugh that makes the stars dance in moonlight.

See the thing is, you have to be home for yourself, you have to see your own worth and know so deeply that every piece of you deserves to be loved.

You have to believe with everything in you that to lose someone like you would be the loss of a lifetime.

Blinded by Pleasure.

As many times as you called me beautiful
I didn't believe it
because I knew that you were
just talking about my body
But I needed you to tell me that my mind
was beautiful
To hear that my intelligence mattered and my
thoughts were worth something
I needed to know that you were in love
with the entirety of who I was
Not just my body and the way it made you feel

<u>Holy.</u>

only a holy man is worthy to step inside the
cathedral that holds her heart.

Fireflies.

You have a billion little fireflies glowing around
your soul,
they bring your inner light to the surface.
These little fireflies have wings thinner than paper,
yet they carry themselves constantly.
Magic is their first language and humility is their
best characteristic.
Much like you, their light is forever behind them,
never able to see the full power of their glow.
But I promise you, it's there.

Your Art.

I hope one day you find your art.

Whatever it is you choose that rests you,

releases you,

refreshes you,

revives you.

I hope you dive deep into it and let it come to life in the form it needs to.

I hope you realize that your art is the material equivalent of your soul and the pieces you share with the world will be the foundation of the magnitude of miracles that come from your existence.

Choices.

opportunities are a lot like breezes

some good, some bad

but if you don't open the window to receive it,

you'll never know.

Feel.

Right now is messy, confusing, bitter, lonely.
I can't wait to fly and still feel grounded,
to come home to a space that feels like mine,
to love people who reciprocate
both the feeling *and* the act,
to feel like the body I live in is a body that stays
strong through every heartache.
I can't wait for the day where I can say I made it.
Because when I reach that day, I will know that
I have finally conquered the things that held me
down.
And I will get there.

6/24.

she's so tired and weak
her heart hurts without reason and
her mind marvels at the defeat
she feels every day.
the unbreakable girl is breaking now.

Even the Best Ones.

I think what frustrates me the most is that you didn't even see yourself leaving.

You didn't see the change in the everyday moments we had.

You didn't pay attention to the amount of times you hurt my heart at the expense of nothing.

You didn't lean into a deeper understanding of my pain and how you could've so easily not been the one causing it.

You didn't follow through with the things you told me you understood so well and thanked me for bringing to the surface.

You didn't think to think about me until you had pushed the limit one too many times.

And maybe you did see yourself leaving but you just didn't care anymore because...how could anyone not leave someone like me?

But when I think about what truly left me ruined in the end, I finally realize that it was my fault.

I had been so aware of these things with such a strong hope that the outcome wouldn't weigh so heavy on my chest like it had the past few months.

What really ruined me is that for so long I had felt nothing, so I was okay with the hurt you were causing.

Whether I deserved it or not (I didn't), I was willing to lay down my heart just to feel the pain...
to feel anything at all.

Insecure.

There are days where my heart is so shaken, so
unsteady.
And I just wish time would stand still.
I wish the moment wasn't what it is and that maybe
I could be in a different life.
I wish to be the girls I see on Instagram with their
model bodies and perfect white smiles.
The ones who seem like they have so much joy, and
so many friends.
I wish to be anything but me,
anywhere but here.
I wish to not have to fight myself every day to keep
pushing.
And more than anything, I wish that my heart would
settle, and finally be secure in the place that it's in.
In *my* chest...*with me.*

<u>Magic.</u>

honey, you are your own magic.

Witness.

Who broke you down so much that you aren't able
to see your light?
Who told you that the stars living in your soul did
not shine bright enough?
Who told you that the shimmer that courses through
your veins does not carry beauty with every move
you make?
Listen love, they were wrong.
Let's pull back the clouds because you are the
brightest glow of sun, moon, and stars,
and the world needs to see your light.
We need you.

When Life Starts to Matter.

Sometimes I crave the peaceful learning moments. You know - the ones where you sit alone in your room and light a candle and you make the atmosphere good and warm. And then read a book or listen to a podcast or watch a Youtube video of someone who's lived a little more life than you.

Sometimes I crave the moments of dancing wild and free and claiming life in a body that was lifeless an hour ago. Sometimes I crave the moments of security...where I roll up like a burrito and watch a movie and everything around me feels cozy and I can get lost in the comfort.

Sometimes I crave the moments of relief and contentment. When I'm driving, and I roll the windows down, the wind is in my hair and the air in my lungs is clear.
Relief because I know this time I have is what refreshes my mind, body, and soul.
Contentment because I know that my heart will not be anywhere but here in this moment.
I'll be present in it for a while and it's okay that I'll have to face reality again when it's done.

Sometimes I crave that really uncomfortable twist in your stomach, "I think I might be sick", not gonna get through it feeling. When reality really slaps you in the face. I know, this one might sound odd...but it's true because that sickness passes, and you always get through it don't you? I crave this moment because I know I'm going to be stronger on the other side, and because that sick feeling is where I learn. When growth punches you in the gut and wisdom floods over your next bad decision.

Sometimes I crave the moments with friends and family where the laughs are so real and so good it hurts...literally. The joy is genuine, the smile is subliminal. Light is shining through and you're finally seeing it.

Sometimes I crave the moments of confusion, and lots of questions, and the need to know *why*. This is where I get to dive deep into my own mind and into others. When I have childlike wonder and the question turns to exclamation. And sometimes the questions have lots of different answers or no answer at all to remind me I'm only human.

All the time, I crave the moments when I see the goodness in each of these things.

Because this is where you see that the good things are coming, and strength is built, honesty is laid out, the heart starts to heal, life means something, and your own life starts to matter.

Advantage.

You've always had the upper hand,
in the way that you are so
unapologetically you

With a smile that would make lightning flinch
and an energy so good that skyscrapers would
shrink themselves just to be next to you

Break.

It's okay to break sometimes,

apart

open

up

down

However you need to, it's okay.

The Dancer.

He fixated on the way my body
moved like the sea.
Claimed my voice was that of an angel
when I would speak.
But these were not the words of the heart
inside of me.

I gave him a song for a smile
and a body for a personality,
because my skin is all that he
really wants to know.
But inside I feel chained to this image
wanting so desperately to break free.
They'll never dive deeper,
they only want a show.
Delicate curls framed the broken smile on my face,
affection and praise flooded the room.
I'm put on this pedestal and told to
achieve a sexy version of grace.
I am adored like an animal in a cage,
not a bride to her groom.

The storm in my soul flowed beautifully
out of my body with every move.
So many eyes looking at me
with fire for what they saw...but did they
really see me?
Another innocent girl objectified,
being told she has something to prove.

Contradictions.

Some days I have unshakable confidence,
and other days I am scared I will never be enough.

<u>Rare.</u>

I hope you discover the magic living in every single
cell that makes up your being.

It is so beautifully rare.

Woman.

She is all sides of this world.

Give her time to recover…

She has taken every beating to make sure all you know is gentle love.

Carried darkness under her skin to let you see nothing but sunshine.

She has laughed the good laugh in the madness to remind you it's gonna be okay, and she has cried tears you will never know the stories of.

Her bones are good, strong, those of a champion.

The mountains thank her for her grace and humility as she is the most glorious one of all.

Do not try to climb her if you don't have the grit to make it to the top,

she is worthy of the same perseverance and strength she gives every day.

Viewpoint.

the mirror you keep looking in is cracked,
and this is why every time you look,
you see a broken girl.
but if you get a new mirror
you will see that you are whole.
all of your dreams, your peace, the love you so
deeply desire…
it is all inside of you already.
you are whole,
the only thing that is still broken
is your idea of beauty.

Alive.

It's time to chase the things that are good for you.
Let sunshine flood your soul as if it was rain.
Dance on waves like the water is strong enough to
hold the magnificent being you are.
Dream with passion so deep it haunts your fears.
Live wildly,
The chaos of your messy life has never looked so
collected like it does when you are doing the things
that make you feel alive.

Natural.

I'd like to write about good things more often,
but the truth of the matter is, I write what I know.
I have not known good long enough to make words
sound beautiful to her ears.

I have known defeat, violence, chaos, brokenness.
I've known these things my entire life.
So while I can write a book about the hurt, I can
barely write a sentence about the good.

Truth.

even mountains are intimidated by you...if only you could see how incredible you truly are.

Necessary.

know the light that burns in your soul
the fierce heart that lives in security underneath the
bones in your chest
the strength that holds your mind together even on
your weakest days
the skin that has been graceful enough to move and
expand throughout every season
this is you, every piece
broken, whole, somewhere in the middle...it doesn't
matter
every piece is necessary,
you are necessary

I Hope They See Your Greatness.

You are the girl with the wings.

Not just the ones tattooed on your wrist.

You are the girl with the wings who showed me
what it feels like to fly,
to laugh until I sob,
to dance until my body hurts,
to believe my light burns as big as bonfires when all
I feel like is a firefly.

The girl with the wings sees the world for what it is,
simple and rough,
but she lives every moment as though she is soaring
to sunsets.

She doesn't always see the greatness she holds in
her wings, the weight she carries, or the magic she
brings to every moment.
Sometimes she lets her feathers fall,
but she is soft to the hardest of hearts, and she'll
listen even though she feels helpless.
She loves deeply and without question.
The girl with the wings is wild, and real, and mad.
Never stop flying…
You've got so much to offer this world.

Climbing

Mountains

Falling Apart.

I've started to put pieces of myself outside of my
walls
but I can't get back on the inside when I need to
When I feel too naked,
and the moment is too vulnerable
My heart begins to shake and everything inside my
skin feels like it's collapsing to the ground

I feel like my soul is being choked from inside my
body when my heart is outside of my walls

<u>Replaced.</u>

Maybe this time I'll learn to accept my place in the
past.
I return to the backseat of your life
day in and day out,
thinking maybe this time the distance
will affect you,
but deep down I know it won't because
someone else is already filling the space.

I'm okay though - It's okay, it's time for change.

Ghosts.

I feel the ghosts in my body when I lay awake at
night staring at the walls.
Somehow always opening the doors of my mind
that I keep locked,
they take everything out of me and pour
chaos back in.
I can feel them when my stomach turns to knots and
the tears are lumped in the back of my throat instead
of my eyes.

They show up every night, without fail.
Clouding my body, making me feel like my skin is
too tight to hold the madness they bring with them.
They haunt me 'til I'm numb.

Losing.

the cement will start to crack and the bricks will
loosen
the walls are losing their steadiness
....I am losing my steadiness
breaking more each day until I am nothing
I am not even me

The Fault.

Her heart was solid gold,
and still,
everyone treated her like silver.

Dotted Lines.

the difference between you feeling connected when
you read the words I write, and me writing these
words because I feel so overwhelmingly
disconnected.

While Dreaming.

broken from reality but the intensity is the same
my mind is spinning inside my skull
the motion pictures created send the feeling through
my veins to my heart
clouded vision...
I can see again

my heart drops and my breathing grows rapid
I can't see anything back here in reality
in reality I feel nothing

It's Not Getting Better.

There aren't a whole lot of words left to say,
the past few weeks have broken me down.
I always come back to the same thought...this is not
the place I was meant to be.
I am weak and tired.

19 years I have walked next to people and still, I am
not seen.
10 years I have tried to fit the unattainable mold
placed in front of me by people who gain security in
my lack of it.
6 years of building and breaking, building and
breaking walls that even when numbingly cold,
were still my home.
3 years of writing words that I pray will stick with
people only for them to forget when they're done
reading.
2 years of recovering, relapsing, refining.

See, the problem is this, people tell you that you
need to tell them what's wrong in order for things to
get better
but in my experience, they just want to have a piece
of your heart without intending to do the long term
work required to keep it.
So here I am with no more air left in my lungs to
repeat myself for people who didn't care the first
time.
Maybe now my silence will be deafening,
maybe now you will see me when you witness my
absence.

Push.

at the end of the day, you have to realize that your
biggest enemy will be the voice in your brain
creating limits for yourself to prevent that feeling of
failure.
the hardest person you'll have to stand up to will be
you, and the pain you face will make you
unstoppable.

The Difference.

no matter how good your heart is, you have to stop
reaching out and letting people have it so easily,
because the reality is people only want you when
they want you.
and wanting someone always when they want you
some of the time will always leave you wondering
why you weren't good enough.
every. single. time.

you are the love light people are searching for, they
just don't know it yet.
there are a lot of people in your life who don't give
you half of what you give them,
keep fighting...but also, stop holding on.

be the person who shows up for people.
even when you don't have the time, or you're crazy
busy, or you're tired...
be strong enough to show up when they need you.
be strong enough to not be held down by their
inconsistency.

Lighter.

Let's go to a place where it
doesn't all feel so heavy.

Forgiveness.

Forgiveness is such a frustrating word and such a
confusing action.
Where love and hate collide
Entirely difficult, entirely necessary
But I will learn to forgive you because time after
time your words and actions remain unchanged.
The words that used to give my heart hope trumped
by the actions that followed and completely
defeated me.

And after I forgive you, I will forgive myself.
I will forgive the part of me that beats and bruises
my soul for not learning the lesson the first time.

I Don't Know Why.

I've always had this problem
with things being *enough*.
myself.
moments.
this life.
And I'm sorry for all of the times people
have given me so much to hold onto and
I claimed that it was not enough.

I don't know why my head does that,
I can't figure out exactly why I feel like something
is missing even when I have everything.
I am so disconnected from myself,
detached from whatever it is I need for it
all to be enough.
Each day the links between my head and
my heart are breaking because they are not tough
enough.

<u>Words for my Friend J: Part 1</u>

You don't have to force yourself to get through it,
because we already know you will.
Just live in it. This is life, it hurts sometimes,
but we need to experience the hurt.
We need to be broken down, uprooted,
and planted again.
We need to be watered every day...even when we
don't want to be...we need to allow *all* the things to
happen.
We need to be able to *go* through it instead of
always trying to get through it.
We need to keep growing,
by whatever means necessary.

Anxiety Again.

I can't stop thinking but I don't even know what
I'm thinking about. My heart is shaking and at the
same time, it feels like ice.

My arm is starting to hurt and there's no real reason
why, but the rest of my body is going numb.

My bones are locked in my skin so much so that I
can't feel anything at all.

I can breathe but barely.

It's this but it's not and it's not but it is.

I feel like there is war inside my skin.

And right now my body does not exist.

And I am not real.

And it just keeps going in and out and it hits so hard
and the panic is suffocating me and I'm so scared.

There's something in my head and I don't know
what it is but it's wrecking me and I feel like a
child again.

A little kid who is too afraid to turn out the lights or
close their eyes because the monsters will get them.

And again, I remember that I am still shaking.

Growing Pains.

the hurt in your heart is only capable of being
healed if you want it to be.

A Mad Perspective.

Sometimes relationships don't work out.

They just don't.

Maybe it's the timing or maybe we just aren't supposed to fit together like we constantly force ourselves to.

Three years later and I can see now that it's not supposed to be like this anymore,

And I hate that I'm breaking you because I really did love you, but I feel like I am cracking now.

I don't feel like myself around you anymore.

When I'm not with you, I don't feel like there's a part of me missing,

I don't get the sparks in my chest or the butterflies-in-my-stomach feeling like I used to.

All too often, I am pulling parts of myself to a love that is not pulling me back.

I lost myself in the middle of the mess, but I need to find my soul again.

And neither one of us are to blame, but I am tired of forcing myself to ignore the fact that I am numb to it all.

I know I am hurting you,

I'm sorry.

But we were both made for more than this...

Made for more than a love that was not made for us.

Loneliest Place.

being on the outside of yourself is so much worse
than being on the outside of anything
to be so guarded and protected that you don't even
know your own heart and mind

people ask you why you're so closed off and you
don't have an answer because you can't even reach
within your heart deep enough to find it
you just keep hitting walls

The Healing Factor.

I think we're all just looking for something to hold
us when we feel like healing is too far away
a person, a thing, a moment.
something that will remind us that we will be okay.
just searching for whatever it is that will carry us
through when the hurt makes a home within us.

Stranger.

I see a stranger when I look in the mirror,
and I'm sorry to all the people who see
pieces of me that I don't.
Thank you for catching the broken bits
before they hit the ground.

Maybe one day the mirror won't show me
all the cracks I've acquired,
and the reflection in it will be
a little more familiar.

<u>Help.</u>

I can't think my own thoughts
my head is empty, yet somehow feels so full
I don't want to be here
you're not okay
I don't want to be here
you're not okay
- repeat -

<u>Ironic.</u>

funny how you said 'always' but what you really
meant was when it's convenient for you.

Racism.

Let's talk about Racism

Let's talk about the "white is right" mentality

Let's talk about how the darker the melanin, the more dangerous the person is

Let's talk about the oppression faced by innocent people for over 100 years

Let's talk about the charges that don't fit the crime

Let's talk about all the "I can't breathes" that went ignored

Let's talk about why it's easier for you to stand in your white supremacy, while you shoot the gun, and beat them into the ground, and steal the air that gives them life

Maybe these things feed your adrenaline, or maybe they just suppress your irrational fear that someone who is dark in color makes them more dangerous at heart

Truth is, I'll never understand

I'll never know why the world celebrates diversity while at the same time taking people out for not being more like them

I'll never be able to comprehend the idea that we are supposed to be "one nation under God" as long as "one nation" means divided and armed to kill, and "under God" means we don't have to surrender our pride for His plan

I will never know why Google knows what it means to be human better than the ones living in this world

I will never grasp the concept that to some people, "Protect and Serve" means kill people for no reason

Let's talk about why it's easier for a man to take another mans life than it is to simply just let him live it

<u>Grace.</u>

Give yourself a little grace,

you have no idea how far you've come.

The Shift.

maybe you're not drowning as much as you think
you are
what if the waves are actually building your
muscles and fortifying your spirit
the salt of the situation establishing your immunity
and maybe your eyes are burning and you can't see
quite like you used to
but maybe that's the point
maybe this rough water is the very thing that
satisfies your thirst for a different life

For The One's Who Weren't Allowed To Live Because They Are Black.

I'm sorry they thought they knew your heart when all they saw was your skin.

This is for anyone who lives every day in fear of being treated differently because they are different.
Fact: we are all different.
But what is it about someone's skin that intimidates the world?

What is it about sexuality, politics, economic status, religion - that shakes us more than earthquakes?
What is it about disability, mental illness, personal beliefs, ethnicity...skin color - that makes us forget that before we are any of these things, we are human.
When will we realize that we are the creators of the brokenness encapsulating the world right now...that we are the authors of the hurt our hearts are going through?
When will we realize that love and unity are what moves the mountains we've been struggling to climb on our own?

No man should be afraid to leave his home, afraid to use his voice, afraid to breathe his next breath.

So for anyone who has made someone feel small for owning who they are...

Did you feel more worthy when you called them worthless?
Did you feel more like a man when you saw her body as a sex symbol instead of a home?
Did you feel more rich when you didn't include someone because they were poor?
Did you feel more powerful when you killed him because his skin was black?
Did you feel more safe when you told them that their religion is wrong?

The world has been stained with cold blood and completely wrecked with consequence.

So I have one last question...
Did it make you feel more human when you robbed him of life as if he was not?

Another Wall @ 1:26 a.m.

I am so tired
My body, my soul, my mind, my heart
All of me needs rest, just a couple of minutes to
break and fall apart
For each piece to unfold, a moment to be nothing

I don't think I've ever experienced heartache like I
did tonight
The kind where it feels like there is a literal hole in
your chest
My body felt so hollow, empty
And still, I tried to give whatever I thought was left
of me to someone else
Still, I tried to be there for someone when I, in fact,
felt like I was nowhere at all

<u>Pause.</u>

don't stop playing the game
don't forfeit now
I know it seems impossible to win considering the
amount of hits you've taken in such little time
so pause
take some time to catch your breath, cover your
wounds, regain your energy.
but please, don't give up just yet.
you were built for success.

Lifestyle.

If you keep accepting the negativity as a lifestyle, you will make yourself accustomed to a different kind of hell.

People Always Leave - Part Infinity.

I have nothing left of my soul to give
The flowers have withered down
The sunshine has been blackened by shadows
The fireflies have lost their twinkle
This is because people keep leaving even after they
promise they won't
And because I keep believing them
Because I keep trying to find worth in a life that has
proven worthless

Greater Things.

You will graduate this season of life,
you were meant for greater things.

Guarded.

I don't say much of what I'm thinking
I don't say much at all really
I don't tell people about the trainwreck
of a life I'm living
and I don't tell them how hard I fight to keep doing
this life every day
or how deep inside my head I can get
or how self-destructive I am
or how intensely I feel like nothing matters
I don't say these things out loud
so when I say I need to talk to you
please say it's okay
because I really need to talk to you

Getting Through.

Sometimes you really have to go through it,
but you always get through it.

Surrender.

Depression drains your body
Breaks your spirit
Paralyzes your heart
And floods your mind

Seconds away from seeing nothing but black,
I let myself slip because I'm too tired to fight back.
I need to rest,
I need to stop inhaling clouds of smoke.
Someone take this brick off of my chest,
please just let me go.

Words for My Friend J: Part 2

We're self-destructive people...

but we will not self-destruct in this life.

We will learn to heal.

To find security, and steadiness.

To be uprooted, replanted, and nourished.

The Entirety.

I know there are a lot of words on these pages that
sound sad but I promise life has gotten better.
I am alive and breathing, safe, grounded, growing.
I have learned, filtered, refined, pursued, evolved.
There are so many pieces of me to witness than just
the unfolded brokenness in the words of these
pages.

To The Future You:

You're here, you're alive, you're human...remember that. We are all alone in this life and at the same time, we are all together. We are a community of unique individuals - be unique, be individual.

We all want to discover "who we are", but what does that even mean? We don't like to be labeled but we live by labels.
Just be.
Life is too confusing already before you attempt to define everything and match up to the standards of society.
When you've reached the point of breaking down because you "don't know who you are", pause and re-evaluate.
You've wasted this much time trying to figure it out instead of just being it. You are *you*, with whatever labels, whatever words fit...even if you don't know what they are yet. But more than anything else, you are human - start with that. Give yourself a chance to get to whatever is next, sometimes all you can do in one moment is exist. That is enough.

Once you regain the capacity to take on more, love yourself, and others. Find purpose in community and passion in something. Envision the moment you wake up every day, you get to be a part of this...live for yourself, make this life your own and love yourself all the way through it.

Remember to "go with the flow". I know this is a common saying but there are moments that you will not be able to control. And yes, life is tough, but there is no growth if there is no struggle. Life is going to kick you down in the dirt, laugh in your face, and leave you helpless on the ground. Condition your mind to be solid enough to get through it. It's all in the mentality you have...you are the only one who can make yourself believe that it's all gonna be okay. Life will throw you around, and it's okay if you let it sometimes but eventually you need to get back up, because the only way to get through it is to get through it.

And while you're doing all of these things, don't forget to build relationships -
because when you get to that point where you're lying in the dirt, completely broken down, you're going to need people.

Someone who is going to look at all of your flaws
and all of the crap you've been through and say,
"I'll love you because you're still worth loving."
And when they say that, *please* let them love you.
Stop building up the walls you always do to guard
your heart. You're tired of being broken, I get
that...but let me tell you, all the best things are.
Despite your past and the situations you've
encountered, you are still worthy of love, still
worthy of the life you've been given (you always
have been). You have to take a chance on yourself,
and others. You have to be brave enough to live life
creatively and freely. If nothing else, you are
creative, you are free, you are human.

Too Far Gone.

What a mess

I've lost my mind,

but nobody believes me.

They don't realize how much deeper that sentence
is than the words that make it up.

And I'm sorry that I can't say it any easier but I've
had a lifetime of conversations that went
misunderstood because this mind of mine has a
mind of its own.

Walls and barricades and here I am on the outside
of myself...again.

Don't you get it? You want me to break my walls,
but the walls aren't even mine anymore.

So it's gone now

- lost -

and I don't know how to get it back.

I'm so sorry.

<u>Happy Mother's Day.</u>

This one is for the women who are struggling with infertility,
who lost their little miracle too soon,
who never got to hold the magic they made in their hands.
This is for the ones who never got to have a conversation with their child,
and the ones who have felt called to be a mother but haven't been given the chance yet.

Even in the weight of these things, I see you.
Your patience
Your grace
For the ones who have walked a journey like
this...you *are* a mother. Maybe the strongest of all.

In The Morning.

you've been running around looking tirelessly for
some sort of saving grace that you've almost lost it
all.
come sit at the table,
put food on your plate,
fill your cup again
the morning will come and we can start over,
you're going to be okay.
I promise.

Roots.

you keep me grounded

growing

thank you for caring about me enough to feed my
light and let the darkness fall off when it starts to
suffocate me

thank you for teaching me to hold onto the life
inside of me and let go of what is already dead

Empty Promises.

You can't just tell me you're going to be there and
then not be.

I will foolishly keep reaching out and I will stupidly
keep believing that you'll answer,

and I will always break more when you don't.

Please understand that I have entrusted so many
pieces of myself to you

So when you say you're going to be there,

I'm going to expect you to be.

Hang On.

I know you feel like you're breaking right now but your spark will return. Just please keep hanging on.

Unbreakable

The Hard Part.

The heartbreak hurts the most, but let's face it, it's the easiest part.

The hard part comes when you have to discipline, sweat, starve, and fight for the version of you that is going to walk out on the other side.

It comes when you realize that the most powerful form of love is the kind you have for yourself.

Don't get discouraged though, you are strong.

- a warrior -

Ashes.

Self-destruction

Depression

Anxiety

Sickness

These are my ashes...the things I leave behind while
I am busy being refined.

I am too busy becoming the fire to try to keep alive
what's already been burned out.

Dignity.

I've spent so many years of my life living in this
state of insecurity
Like I couldn't make moves because I was too
scared of failing
I wasted so many years letting the demons in my
mind steal my power
Always letting myself be knocked down too easily,
allowing the insanity to get the best of me

Until one day when I met confidence
She introduced herself as the
strongest weapon I will ever own
I stood up that day
I have not been defeated since

<u>Warrior.</u>

To the ones who are still soft to love
after they've given their heart to
people that give nothing back,
I see you.
You are a force to be reckoned with.

Refined.

I believe good things will come
I will walk through the dark with such strong
confidence like I have never seen so clearly
I will fight with the strength of someone who has
been beaten down so hard and stood back up to take
more
I will love whatever is trying to break me because
giving in to the way of my demons only empowers
them
I will seek peace in the constant hell I am going
through
I will push my limits until I have wrecked the
construction of what this world has built me to be

Underneath all the pain is goodness
Good things are coming
I am a good thing

New Places.

I traveled a lot this year

I looked at pictures of myself and saw a beautiful girl who was learning self-love for the first time.

I walked away from friendships that were no longer helping me grow.

I cultivated relationships with incredible people that spread positivity like wildfire.

I faced opportunities and experiences I was terrified of...and I conquered them.

I went outside of my walls rather than just letting others in.

I woke up each day and called myself worthy.

I claimed freedom from my insecurities and addictions.

I stepped out of my comfort zone and into independence.

I dug into some of the deepest, darkest corners of my mind to see some of the brightest.

I fought like the warrior I am, and I beat each trial like the champion I am becoming.

I traveled a lot this year...and I have found so much life in the places I've been.

Sorry Times A Million.

'Sorry' can't heal the pain you keep inflicting and it doesn't fix the hurtful actions you keep taking.

So I'm walking away now because I know I'm deserving of better than the hurt you've countlessly put me through.

You can apologize a million times, but it doesn't work anymore.

'Sorry' doesn't make the bad actions good.

Unbreakable: Part 1

There used to be so much life inside of me, so many good things.
Except now I give all these things to other people, and always with a smile.
Every day, I collect all my broken pieces and present them as a whole for others to have.

I mean this in the way that I give them the hours-long-heart-talks, and the deep belly laughs.
The "I'm good, how are you?"
The pep talk about hope and how "it gets better", the fascination about life and breath and moon and stars.

I mean this in the way that I break a little more each time I give these things,
Because the heart-talks don't seem to really mean anything once they're over, and the belly laughs were more for show than they were actual joy.
The "I'm good, how are you?" is just another wall, and the speech about hope is not reflected in my own life because I haven't really found it yet...but I want others to.

And because the fascination with the universe is just me secretly questioning if anything really exists.

For a while, I've been believing myself to be unbreakable…
Unbreakable in the sense that no one can tear me down, no one can break my spirit, no one can destroy the life in my bones.
But I now know the core layer of what I really believe when I claim to be unbreakable.
No one else can break me because I have broken myself down as far as I can, I have scraped resilience from my bones and crushed myself into a form completely unrepairable.

Moving On.

I've realized that I am no longer the first person you laugh to, cry to, talk to, turn to.

I witness your greatest moments second hand.

I think about every heart talk, summer sunset, laugh until our ribs are tough moment and how long it's been since the last time we did these things.

We are standing still now and I can feel the ache flood my body, my chest feels like it was beaten in, and my spine is weak from the hurt.

But I know that the hurt is there to tell me that I have succeeded, because I have broken barriers for a love so real in the time that it lasted.

For the first time, I have learned that life makes you move whether you want to or not, and that I am capable of moving on, that I can and will grow from this hurt.

Oceans.

They put you in a box
like you could be contained,
but oceans are not held by walls.

Never Needed You.

I've lived every day in fear of losing people,
unable to open up to someone new because they
might walk away.

But I'm finally at a point now where I'm not afraid
of anyone leaving.
Lately, the people in my life haven't helped me
move, they haven't helped me feel, and they haven't
helped me love.
So I'm okay if they decide to leave, because if I lose
people who have kept me stagnant, I will have
regained an intimacy with the piece of my soul that
keeps whispering, "you deserve to grow".

Skyscraper.

Her heart is strong even when it breaks.

Her mind is stubborn even when the moment is soft.

Her love is deep even when the person is shallow.

Her fight is fierce when the battle is fiercer.

She will set you on fire and let you burn,

and she will not watch you because you are no
longer worth her time.

She is moving on to herself, her passions, and her
purpose.

If she has to constantly balance the flame,

it is not one worth fighting for.

The burn of tonight will never outweigh the
skyscraper she will be tomorrow.

For the Strong Ones.

You harvested grace in every season of life,
and maybe that's why you feel like you're breaking
now.

You have remained so kind and peaceful in the
most destructive of storms.

You have been giving your all for far too long and
have received nothing in return.

Unbreakable: Part 2

I think I'm getting there
To the good version of "unbreakable"
It's never been easy
It's not supposed to be
But I'm finding air again in the places I couldn't
breathe before
Hope in the pieces of my soul that were paralyzed
Home in the body that was always empty

Leaps.

I know what you mean when you say I've got to
take leaps, but understand this…
I am the kind of girl whose anxieties stay silent
while my bones shake inside my skin, and my chest
tightens around my heart like ice.
The type of girl who will smile while her mind is
going through hell, just so you see strength.
This is the girl who tells people, "I will be here for
you, always", while in that exact same moment not
being able to feel her own body and know she
is alive.
She will say "I'm okay" instead of telling you she
doesn't know if she can do it all again tomorrow.
She is guarded, going back and forth between
breaking and being unbreakable - built walls with
everybody and even within herself.

I know what you mean when you say I've got to
take leaps, but before you tell me to leap,
please just help me get up off the ground.

CM's Poem.

"How are you?"

"Exhausted, but still going."

For the girl who walks through fire every single day...

Did you remember to breathe today?

How about making sure the first person you said "I'm here for you" to was yourself?

Did you look in the mirror and recognize your light?

For the world...let me tell you about the girl who walks through fire every single day...

Her soul is drenched in glitter while the shimmer in her eyes is met by passion so deep she roots her purpose in it.

Every day she lives out the very definition of love, and every second she brings it to life.

She laughs in the chaos because she knows the one who made the stars, holds not only her hand but all of her.

She is the girl who doesn't have enough hours in the day to check on her own heart because she is too busy checking on everyone else.
She's got a smile that makes you question if you've ever really known peace and perseverance like she does.

Brave, beautiful, wild, fearless, strong, selfless, consistent, grounded, worthy, a warrior, a winner.

There will never be enough words to encapsulate the entirety of her fire, so for now...
She is the one who walks through fire every single day.
The sparks she creates are ignited through real and raw vulnerability, she burns, shines, and glows even in the darkest nights.
Her bones are made of stardust,
and her heart is made of honey-golden love.
To the woman who walks through fire every day...
CM, you *are* the fire.

The Fight.

I think my weakest moments are also my strongest.
I don't rely on people to fight for me,
I fight for myself and then I get up and fight for
everyone else too.
I am my own rock,
the one reminding myself of the strength I have to
get through the next moment.
We can all be our own strength.

New Seasons.

Life isn't going to stop for you, no matter how bad you may want it to or even if you feel like it needs to. This season you're in is temporary. The hurt, the pain, the brokenness, the laughter, the excitement, the peace is all going to eventually become something entirely new. Life will come at you full force when you feel unequipped to handle it most. The light will shine through when you realize the moment you're living in right now, has been brought to life *by* you. Created, shaped, attracted, received, cultivated, and nourished by you. You have, for so long, been growing the roots for the life you're living, the life that isn't going to stop, the life that you have been given the responsibility to walk through.

For my Good Friend DeLuca.

One day you're going to wake up and you're not going to be so restless about the life you're living. You're going to realize that you have always been where you were meant to be.

You are going to look at life and love yourself for the simple fact that you've made it this far.

You're going to appreciate every breath you take and every next beat of your heart as they come and go.

You will conquer every battle you encounter because you are a fighter.

You're going to love people fiercely and fearlessly, you're going to be confident in your purpose and flourish in whatever it may be.

You're going to be a light in every dark situation because your spirit shines so bright and you don't even know it.

You're going to laugh until you can't breathe and in the back of your mind you'll be thinking, "this is what living the good life means."

And most importantly, when that day comes and you wake up and you're not so restless anymore, you're going to realize that you are no longer the girl you were in high school.

She grew out of you because you grew out of her. You won't want the same things or talk about the same things, or even care to remember her because she is in the past where she belongs, and you are here where you belong.

So remember the outcome...at the end of everything, the only things you're going to have are yourself, the relationships you've cultivated and nourished, and the faith in whatever it is you believe comes after this life.

Make sure these things are good,

make sure these things were as real to you as you were to them.

Rise.

Eventually I learned my strength
I rose as a tidal wave of confidence
Crashing down on your flames
I refuse to be defeated so quick
I am a sea of power

The Reason I'm Still Hanging On.

You saved so much more than a life that day.

You saved my heart, my smile, my laugh, my light, my dark, my words, my mind, my hope.

You saved all the joy I get from the songs I have yet to hear, and the peace I'll experience from every sunset my eyes haven't seen.

You saved all the love I am going to receive and all the people I haven't gotten the chance to love on yet.

For the first time ever, I saw panic in you that had resided in me so many times before.

Body shaking beyond your control and tears in your eyes that you would not let fall. I saw your fear and I realized that just because I couldn't feel didn't mean I didn't have the ability to make others feel.

You saved all the lessons I still have to learn...all the growing I still have to do.

You saved the potential of a life for me that I was blind to for so long.

Please do not think lightly of the hero you were that day...to have the strength you had, staying so collected while picking up all of my broken pieces.

Thank you for believing in me and for carrying me throughout every moment I couldn't do it for myself.

"You are the reason I'm still hanging on."

Shine Bright.

You have fragments of galaxies flowing through your veins as the fire in your soul burns from the inside out.

Look at the sun, the one who has pushed herself to meet the sky every day just to say "good morning."

Just like the bones inside your skin, she has moved consciously and graciously for others.

She was built to be strong -

Strong enough to keep shining.

You were also built to be strong -

Strong enough to keep going.

To keep rising.

10/4/19.

I think sometimes there is beauty in the heartbreak,
in the hurt that comes with loss.

It's beautiful to know that a piece of this world was
loved so deeply by another.

One human treasured by another,
all of the broken pieces somehow connected in two
souls.

And I think too often we only see beauty in the
good times, but there is peace and comfort in
knowing that the destruction of this world doesn't
always win.

Either Way.

when I am bare and stripped of everything that
holds me together is when you will see the real me

when I feel too weak to go on
when I am completely undone
down to the core
it's going to be so dark
so deep
and a little too real
and you're either going to stay
or you're going to leave
but no matter what happens
I will be okay

A Letter to My Body.

Some days I hate you. I hate you so much I want to hurt you. I see you in the mirror in your entirety and I wish I could disappear.

And some days, I think you look really good. When I see that you are so beautiful, powerful...purposeful. There are days I look at you and am amazed by how much I've put you through. How many scraped knees you've conquered, all of the broken bones, how many times the walls have been kicked in, and how many weights you've carried on your chest. Every moment you've taken pain like a champion, and allowed the healing to happen just when it needs to. And all the times you have gone entirely numb, when I couldn't feel you and I didn't know if you were really there but *still* you showed up. You did what I needed you to do - so gracefully, so humbly.

All the tears you tried to cry when I wouldn't let
you and all the power you possessed to hold in the
tears when the time wasn't right. For all of the
times when life has been so heavy and I've used
you as a punching bag for the hell in my head.

You have been through so much more than my
mind will ever understand because the killer never
experiences the pain like the victim does.
I see now just how loyal and unbreakable you have
been all this time.

Keep It Coming.

gratitude is the air that she breathes
because she knows it's the little things that carry her
the little things that keep her from falling
that keep her flying

Kingdom.

the thoughts in my mind burn me every day, they
leave me with scars and steal my sanity.
there are demons sitting on top of angels and there
are so many walls broken,
so many shields laying on the ground.
and the entire time, I have looked at a golden throne
wondering who belongs there, questioning when
someone will come with an anthem of hope.
but I've figured it out now, I've realized how
ludicrous it all is.
this is *my* kingdom.

Not In The Way You Can.

You are meant to be here.

I know it may feel like you are breaking and you want to give in to the hurt, but let me tell you love, no one can carry the weight of your life quite like you do.

No one can exemplify grace in the immensity of an ocean, and no one can hold the stars in their soul and not be burned...not in the way you can.

The bones under your skin are those of a conqueror with ten thousand mountains climbed and the ability to smile in the lowest part of heartache.

A warrior woven from challenge, fear, defeat, passion, strength.

Please keep fighting, this world needs you.

MM's Poem.

You are the reason for so many things.

Dust turns to gold at your fingertips,

this is your art.

Defeat is what drives your dedication,

this is your power.

Love is a language to you and not just a feeling,

this is your beauty.

Look at everything we've done...you and me.

Look at everything we've been through, created,

overcame, seen the light in.

These things are here for you, to remind you of who

you are, everything we are, everything we can (will)

be.

These things are here for the both of us,

they are our reasons,

to make sure we never forget.

Roses.

How did I get here?

How did I get so close to people who don't think twice about walking away?

The roses on my bones are hidden behind a skin wall of thorns.

This is how I keep them growing,

Saving them from being cut off their roots and left to die.

Saving them from being loved when it's convenient to be, and thrown on the ground when they are no longer wanted.

The roses of me don't deserve to be treated like that anymore.

<u>Revolutionary.</u>

why do you spend so much of the time waiting for
him to come around
to love you again
what if you picked up all the pieces and loved them
yourself
loved them anyway
you can be the girl who waits for love or you can be
the girl who is her own love

but the girl who is her own love is already winning

__Differently.__

Just start moving differently,
some people will walk...*you* will soar.
Everything will fall into place,
the confusion will stop, the peace will flow, those
who are truly there for you will show up.
Trust it. Trust you.

Even Still.

I've always had this fear of coming undone.
You know, of falling apart in the places
you're not supposed to,
in front of people you're not supposed to.
I get nervous that I will get too shaken up
in the moment by the circumstance.

But even in my most vulnerable state,
I am still an unbreakable woman.

Battle.

You've been fighting with your fists...it's time to pick up the sword.

2/6/18.

Dear February 6th,

     You were one of my weakest moments. Not necessarily the weakest because every day since then I've experienced something that reminds me of you. I've seen or heard or smelled or been in a state that makes my head spin in a silent storm of anxiety. Every single day I've thought about you, and it's in those moments that I feel even weaker. Each day I feel like I am walking barefoot on burning concrete, suffering through the hurt but forcing myself to get through it because it hurts more to just stand there. But each day I am conquering a little more of this pavement so that maybe one day I will be able to walk on a path I've paved for myself. Where the concrete isn't so hot, and there's some grass in the middle that crunches beneath my toes to remind me that I still have this body when I feel like I have nothing else.

When my heart has fallen, when I am scared of how big the world is, when I think too deeply and everything seems pointless.

When I feel weaker than I did on February 6th, I will at least be reminded that throughout the chaos my mind is in, my body alone is stronger than something. Even if that something is grass,

I will be grounded in it, I will root my soul into the dirt and nourish all of my fears, all of my broken pieces, all of my heartache, all of my weaknesses - to grow a new life.

At 7:26 a.m. I remember not being able to breathe and the tears that didn't leave my skin. This was the first time in my entire life that the tears ran down my neck, they always fall when they hit the bottom of my cheeks but they didn't this time. Why didn't they fall? Maybe to tell me that I am whole even when I am broken. Or that it's okay if I need to hold onto the hurt a little while longer. I remember not being able to explain what was happening. I needed someone to talk to even though I couldn't speak. I remember every person who saw me and said "what's going on?"...I hate those words. I remember the emptiness that controlled my mind, the numbness that overcame my body. And being blind to my future...not hopeless, just blind. I remember the sickness that came in waves, and the way death slowly started to replace life. I remember being trapped in one of my greatest fears - vulnerability. Most of all, I remember the panic, because the panic was the only constant for me that day. The only thing I was able to hold inside my skin no matter how hard I tried to let it go.

Right now, I'm choosing to remember how strong I was...how strong I am. My heart will climb worse mountains than you, my mind will conquer every moment that makes me feel defeated. February 6th, you have scarred my soul more than you have scarred my skin, and *still*, I am stronger.

Sincerely,
the girl who got through it.

(To the ones who were there that day, thank you for helping me get through it and beyond it. Thank you for showing up.)

JM's Poem.

I'm not sure if you'll ever know how much it all means to me - you are the reason I can recollect myself when all hell breaks loose. There aren't words to explain how grateful I am for the moments I've brought the weakest version of myself to you and you've built me to be stronger. Thank you for every conversation, for the time you've invested towards someone so broken with so much faith that she was tough enough to turn it all around. You are the kind of person who opens people's eyes, who speaks life into lifeless situations, breaks walls, keeps it real one hundred percent of the time, and always wants to witness the vulnerability of the hurt rather than the fake smiles. Thank you for being so willing to walk with me through all of my darkness. Throughout every "not enough" and every "I'm tired" you have understood and shown me what it really means to be resilient, to be a fighter.
If you haven't realized it yet, I would not be where I am without you...here,
alive.

Champions are created at your fingertips.

Minds are rebuilt by your words.

Lives are restored in your presence.

You have moved mountains that some are
incapable of even climbing,

and shattered weakness with your fist.

I hope everyone has the chance to meet someone
like you...to *attract* a soul who never gives up the
fight.

The one who can take countless hits and keeps
getting back up.

Thank you for your willingness to listen, your
desire to be present, your passion to free a mind that
is suffocating in the madness. Even when I've lost
it, you've reminded me that I am not too far gone.
You and I see the world through a very different
lens, but that's a good thing - we know.

JM, I wrote this for you, because *you* are the one
who has helped me take the ashes of who I was and
turn it into something...someone, so incredibly
unbreakable. Thank you.

Underdog.

I found the dog inside of me,
the one who can't be shaken.
I found this fight in my soul that refuses to give up,
refuses to back down,
and goes harder when the weight gets stronger.
I found the one who has been through hell and back,
ready to do it again.
Who does not fall victim to anything life throws,
but keeps playing the game to walk out a champion.

please continue; +

Made in the USA
Middletown, DE
16 December 2020